where your treasure is

A LIFE-QUESTION DEVOTIONAL READER

How Are My Investments Doing?

Prepared by
David A. Staff, *Lead Pastor*
Christ Community Church of Ames, IA

TABLE OF CONTENTS

4   **INTRODUCTION**
Salvation. Stewardship. Where my treasure is.

9   **ONE** MY TREASURE: The Genesis of Stewardship
Genesis 4

15   **TWO** MY TREASURE: First Fruits Consistency
Exodus 23, Prov. 3:9-10, Luke 6:38

21   **THREE** MY TREASURE: Understanding Tithing
OT/NT Scriptures

27   **FOUR** MY TREASURE: Where is it?
Matthew 6:19-23, Luke 12:13-21

33   **FIVE** MY TREASURE: Which is it?
Matthew 6:24, 1 Timothy 6:9-10

39   **SIX** MY TREASURE: God's Promises
Matthew 6:25-33, Philippians 4:10-20

45   **SEVEN** MY TREASURE: Faithfully Generous
Mark 12:41-44, 2 Corinthians 8-9

51   **EIGHT** MY TREASURE: The Rewards of Stewardship Investing
Luke 12:41-48, 19:11-17, Matthew 25:14-30

59   **NINE** MY TREASURE: The Quicksand Of Debt
Romans 13:8, Proverbs 22:7

65   **TEN** MY TREASURE: Stewardship as a Family
Various Scriptures

70   **CONCLUDING WORD**
Generosity and Kingdom Investing

72   Life Question "How Are My Investments Doing?" focus
Evaluation-Growth Tool

73   Acknowledgements

Introduction

Salvation

For weeks I had struggled with fear and doubt. Sunday night worship services at Calvary Memorial Church (Racine, Wisconsin) had featured preaching on the return of Jesus, and the rapture of those who were ready.

I wasn't.

I knew it, though I had been born and raised in that wonderful, Bible teaching church. Still, since standing in a garage fails to magically turn one into an automobile, my attending church since childhood had not automatically made me a Christian. My grandparents and my parents had walked with God. I had not yet found the pathway. God has no grandchildren.

Finally, late one evening, under the conviction of God's Holy Spirit, I knelt on our green carpet in our modest living room. With elbows propped on the cushions of our orange coach, head bowed, I acknowledged that Jesus had died in my place, for my sins, and asked him to fully forgive me.

Dad was traveling on business. Again, Mom patiently made the gospel clear late that evening when the Spirit would not let me sleep. My salvation needed to be settled. When my simple prayer of faith concluded, I felt the first effects of forgiveness. It was like a large rock had been lifted from my chest.

> **WHEN ANYONE REPENTS AND TRUSTS IN JESUS, IT IS GOD WHO REJOICES EVEN AS THE ANGELS LOOK ON.**

My mother also quickly pointed out that there was now a party going on in heaven (cf. Luke 15:7,10). She said the angels were rejoicing because I had trusted in Jesus. A wandering sheep rescued; a lost coin found. Later in life I looked closer at those verses, noting there was "rejoicing in the *presence* of the angels of God" (KJV). It was God doing the rejoicing, as the heaven's angels looked on. This even more compelling.

It was one of those seminal moments which changed my life. I was 9 years old. I was forgiven, and I was ready for Jesus' momentary return.

(I still am, by the enduring grace of God.) Early on I began my following of Jesus reading (indeed devouring) a gift, a copy of *The Scofield Reference Bible* my parents gave me two months later on my 10th birthday. Through my years in public education, I would include it in the books I carried to school, to read it between classes, or at lunch.

On December 31, 1965, I publicly acknowledged my faith at a New Year's Eve baptismal service. I had died and been raised with Christ. It was time to seriously follow Him with my life.

Stewardship

Over time, with three kids needing more room, my parents decided to finish a portion of our basement which would become my new bedroom.

Ours was not a wealthy family. Dad often worked part-time jobs, one in the morning and another in the evening, bookending a regular day job at a local print shop.

I remember we started getting new things. New carpet. A small organ for mom to play at home (she played for our worship ministry at church). A new detached double garage. Some nice improvements. And what middle schooler asks financial questions? All the stuff was nice.

One night however, dad came down to my room in the basement. I was trying to go to sleep, and was surprised when he came in and sat on the edge of the bed.

"David," he said, "I need to tell you something."

"OK," I replied, not knowing what was coming.

> WHEN DAD LEFT, I REALIZED HOW IMPORTANT IT WAS TO MAKE THIS STEWARDSHIP PROMISE TO HIS SON.

"I've gotten our family into debt, wanting to get mom and our family nicer things. But I've not been handling the money God provides for us well, and we haven't been giving to the Lord."

I'm not sure I said anything, waiting for what was next.

"I just wanted to tell you that the Lord is going to come first from now on. The first 10% will go to the Lord, and Lord willing, if we honor Him, He'll help us get out of debt. OK?"

When dad left, I realized it was important to my father to make a promise to his son. Such a promise to God and to me was a discipleship decision for my father. I would later realize that Mom would start managing the finances, and knowing her level of conviction about obeying the Lord, the first-fruits tithe would rarely (if ever) be missed.

That night was another seminal fork-in-the-road moment for me, and more broadly for our entire family. It took a while, but eventually, the Lord honored my father's decision and my parents' follow through. Putting the Lord first meant our needs were always met, and in due season, our family climbed out of debt.

A true story to treasure.

Let Salvation Result In Stewardship

In Luke's account of Jesus' Sermon on the Mount (Luke 6), the Savior lists a number of personal practices which evidence a true relationship with his Father. Often, the spotlight is on generously using the resources He places in our hands.

> *Luke 6:27-38* "But I say to you who hear, Love your enemies, do good to those who hate you, bless those who curse you, pray for those who abuse you. To one who strikes you on the cheek, offer the other also, and from one who takes away your cloak do not withhold your tunic either. Give to everyone who begs from you, and from one who takes away your goods do not demand them back. And as you wish that others would do to you, do so to them.
>
> "If you love those who love you, what benefit is that to you? For even sinners love those who love them. And if you do good to those who do good to you, what benefit is that to you? For even sinners do the same. And if you lend to those from whom you expect to receive, what credit is that to you? Even sinners lend to sinners, to get back the same amount. But love your enemies, and do good, and lend, expecting nothing in return, and your reward will be great, and you will be sons of the Most High, for he is kind to the ungrateful and the evil. Be merciful, even as your Father is merciful.
>
> "Judge not, and you will not be judged; condemn not, and you will not be condemned; forgive, and you will be forgiven; give, and it will be given to you. Good measure, pressed down, shaken together, running over, will be put into your lap. For with the measure you use it will be measured back to you."

His instruction exudes a spirit of generosity, flowing from the character and heart of a God who is a giving Father. His love is more than a feeling of affection; it is demonstrated in actions which bless and benefit

— indeed renew — our lives.

Yet even more, there is promise attached to obedience which is generous. God promises reward for demonstrating, tangibly toward others, that we are "sons of the Most High." And our generous giving is connected to receiving what we need, and even more (Luke 6:38). Furthermore, such obedient stewardship is a building of one's "house" (or life) on "the rock," a building which withstands the frequent storms of life's travails (Luke 6:46-49). Conversely, to disobey is to foolishly neglect laying any solid foundation under one's house.

Where My Treasure Is

Our Savior and Lord knows us. He knows we struggle swimming in a culture which frequently trumpets experiencing what it calls "the good life." It encourages relentless spending on yourself, on current pleasures, on feeding what the Scripture identifies as our "flesh." The wisdom from below urges investing here, and mostly for self, despite both Scriptural (and sometimes market) warnings that thieves can break in and steal our assets, that moth and rust quickly corrupts the diminishing value of our possessions.

OUR HEART FOLLOWS WHERE WE PLACE OUR TREASURE.

Jesus knows we struggle with fear over controlling what we have in our grasp. Corrie Ten Boom once said, "I have learned to hold all things loosely, so God will not have to pry them out of my hands." His antidote for a clutching habit is to raise our eyes toward the future endowment of life in the coming age, in His Kingdom.

> *Luke 12:32-34* "Fear not, little flock, for it is your Father's good pleasure to give you the kingdom. Sell your possessions, and give to the needy. Provide yourselves with moneybags that do not grow old, with a treasure in the heavens that does not fail, where no thief approaches and no moth destroys. For where your treasure is, there will your heart be also.

Our heart follows where we place our treasure. Invest treasure here on earth, and our hearts will be earth-bound, self-focused. Invest treasure in eternal causes, and in people generously, and our hearts will be found pulsating with the life of God's kingdom, anticipating eternity.

Where is your treasure? Where are you investing the treasure that God (who gives us everything) gives you?

This devotional reader seeks to encourage a holy, generous stewardship habit of investing in eternal endeavors, in keeping with our mission to "connect people to life-defining relationships in Christ."

The 6th life question for disciples at Christ Community Church (Ames, IA) asks, **"How are my investments doing?"** As stewards of God, endowed with time, gifts and talents, strength and energy, and financial resources, we evaluate our investing in eternity.

Our 4th ministry value is **radical generosity: living adventurously to impact our world.**

May the Spirit of God speak well to each of us about this key area in following Jesus. May we eagerly not only call Jesus "Lord," but do the things which he says (Luke 6:46).

David A. Staff
December 2020

ONE

MY TREASURE

The Genesis of Stewardship

Genesis 4

The creation of the universe and our earthly home as its centerpiece was a majestic event that defies description in known language. Even our most vivid imaginings fall short. The Spirit's Biblical narrative of the handiwork movements of God compels worship, urging a response of thankful humility (cf. Romans 1:20-21). But the Hebrew texts of Genesis 1-3 are so very brief, inciting great curiosity, a longing for additional clarity.

Yet very clear is that the crowning act of creation was man, himself and herself, two human beings *uniquely* fashioned in the image of God. "In the image of God He created him, male and female He created them" (Genesis 1:27).

Perfect though in untested holiness, Adam and Eve immediately possessed an endowment, the challenging stewardship of a flourishing garden on the land of planet earth, a ball of life postured midst galaxies proclaiming the glory of God. The couple was to dance with God through loving, eager obedience in managing and developing all of the world's untapped resources. Young regents, called as overseers, within God's fresh kingdom-creation.

All they needed to do was trust and obey.

Tragically, Genesis 3 records the chosen disobedience, a fall unleashing Pandora's box of sin and consequences, both inside the human heart and spreading throughout all the physical creation. Everything created was now, and suddenly, compromised by the progressive degeneration of death. Whole-hearted, godly stewardship of God's endowed resources suddenly became a battle, a fight, a personal struggle. In the midst of plenty, a selfish, independent satisfaction of the flesh became the human default.

Generosity with God and with others would happen only as human beings leaned humbly back toward their generous Creator in thankful worship. As Genesis records, some would, while others (eventually, most!) would not.

The Stewardship Of Cain And Abel

Recovering from the loss of expulsion from the Garden of Eden, Eve one day gleefully shouted, "I have gotten a man with the help of the Lord" (Genesis 4:1). The mother of all the living, recognized what Psalm 127:3 would echo, "the fruit of the womb is His reward." Cain was her firstborn, with the Lord helping again in the safe delivery of a 2nd son, named Abel. In time, these two found their niche—Abel a keeper of sheep, Cain a farmer working the soil.

We don't know how they came to understand a rhythm of worship (perhaps Adam and Eve instilled a "rest on the 7th day" family habit). What we are told is that "in the course of time" both young men brought an offering from the fruit of their labors. Somehow, they got the picture that acknowledging the hand of the Lord in the success of their work was necessary.

Yet the boys came with very different gifts. Different not merely in what was given, but what the gift itself communicated to the Lord.

The elder brother, Cain, simply discharged a duty. He brought "some" of the fruit of the ground. He had to do his thing, so it seems, for God. So he quickly scooped up something and made an appearance.

The younger brother, Abel, went out of his way to give the Lord the best. He brought "of the firstborn of his flock and of their fat portions." Not just a left-over animal, but an offering from the fattest, or the healthiest, of his entire herd. The animal that would have brought the highest price at the market. Indeed Abel offered the best parts of the best animal.

Immediately, God knew each man's attitude and motivation, knowledge confirmed in the Spirit's assessment in Hebrews 11:4. "By faith Abel offered to God a more acceptable sacrifice than Cain, through which he was commended as righteous, God commending him by accepting his gifts. And through his faith, though he died, he still speaks."

> **CAIN ALWAYS GAVE WHAT WAS LEFT OVER. ABEL ALWAYS OFFERED WHAT WAS BEST.**

Notice, if you will, the plural "gifts." Abel did this more than once, and perhaps Cain as well. Each man coming to offer an expression of faith and thankfulness. One always with what was left over while the other always with the best.

God's response? He had "no regard" for Cain and what he brought. Yet as Abel worshipped, God had regard "for Abel and his offering" (Genesis 4:5). The wording of the text merits mining, as God looks first at the man himself (at his heart, if you will) and then at what he brought. What's inside is expressed through what is outside. Abel was commended as righteous, Cain as unrighteous.

Beginnings Set The Standard

Lessons from these brothers, worshipping God at the dawn of human history, are more critical than what we might casually think. The earliest life lessons in Scripture are all about stewardship. From Cain we learn that someone going through the motions alone — especially religious motions — merits no commendation before God. Cain is the posterchild of insincerity. From him no one should assume that God is ever satisfied with merely a show of religion. Rather, the Lord is always and immediately aware when we try to pass off second rate love or thankfulness toward Him. Centuries later, David reminds Solomon "the Lord searches all hearts and understands every plan and thought" (1 Chronicles 28:9).

When it comes to stewardship, either we keep our treasure (the best of what we produce) and give God "some," or we give our treasure offering God the first and the best. Cain believed mediocrity could pass muster with God. It couldn't. Never does.

From Abel we learn the joy of giving to God the first and the best, from a heart that realizes that everything we have comes from Him. Though Abel's life was cut short by Cain's angry, murderous jealousy, Abel becomes, notably, the first name in Hebrews 11's faith hall-of-fame. His stewardship voice remains powerful, heard clearly in any generation if we have ears to hear.

"Of the firstborn of the flock, and of their fat portions." **Stewardship that is righteous brings treasure that is of the first and of the best.** Giving that way brings the regard of God.

REFLECTION AND DISCUSSION QUESTIONS

What is the lesson I am hearing from the contrasting stewardship of Cain and Abel?

Which one of these first two sons reflected "radical generosity"?

In light of this, how would I evaluate how and what I bring to the Lord? Do I always bring the first and the best? If not, what do I bring and why? Do my worship/giving habits need an upgrade?

TWO

MY TREASURE

First Fruits Consistency

Exodus 23, Proverbs 3:9-10, Luke 6:38

Here's one thing I've observed over decades of shepherding thousands of people. Most people care deeply about what others think about them. Most of us want to be thought of well. Our reputation, our standing in the community, being perceived as a thoughtful, caring person, welcomed and sought out by others — these social, interpersonal markers matter.

So when's the last time you gave any thought to what God thinks when He thinks about you? How does He size you up? Does He smile when you come to mind? Delight in you as His child? Is He eager for your company, and anxious that you do well as life unfolds?

Some may respond more negatively to these kinds of questions. Such a response often comes from those who struggled to secure the approval and joy of their own parents. Negativity and criticism clouded the atmosphere of the home. You were simply never "good enough," even on your best days.

Enough already! You're a Christian!! Born into a new family with a perfect Heavenly Father. And here is what He thinks of you. You are a kind of "first fruits" of all that He has created. James is moved to put it this way:

> *James 1:17-18*   Every good gift and every perfect gift is from above, coming down from the Father of lights, with whom there is no variation or shadow due to change. Of his own will he brought us forth by the word of truth, that we should be a kind of firstfruits of his creatures.

Paul speaks similarly about the believers in Thessalonica.

> *2 Thessalonians 2:13*   But we ought always to give thanks to God for you, brothers beloved by the Lord, because God chose you as the firstfruits to be saved, through sanctification by the Spirit and belief in the truth.

John is given a glimpse of those following the Lamb during difficult days of world-wide trouble.

> *Revelation 14:4*   It is these who have not defiled themselves with women, for they are virgins. It is these who follow the Lamb wherever he goes.   These have been redeemed from mankind as firstfruits for God and the Lamb.

Again, Paul employs the firstfruits imagery speaking of the primacy of Christ in his resurrection, to encourage the hope of all who would follow him out of death.

> *1 Corinthians 15:23*   But each in his own order: Christ the firstfruits, then at his coming those who belong to Christ

The Significance of First Fruits

In both Old Testament Scripture and in Hebrew thought, the "first fruits" of the annual harvest were always considered the best. Accordingly, the first child born in a family, the first fleece shorn from the sheep, the first of the wine from a vineyard, the first of the oil produced, the first grains from the field, the first crop from the fruit trees — the first was thought to be both primary and special.

Used metaphorically as a descriptor for New Testament era believers, Christians are considered by their heavenly Father to be the first and best among all humanity, a kind of "firstfruits for God and for the Lamb."

Thus in the precedent originally set by Abel's offering (cf. Genesis 4:4), Old Testament Law directed that a grateful worshipper bring the first fruits of his labor to the Lord, to express his/her joy and thankfulness. At the annual Feast of Harvest (Exodus 23:16), first fruit offerings were presented. "The best of the firstfruits of your ground you shall bring to the house of the Lord your God" (Exodus 34:26).

The Levitical priests were to regularly receive firstfruit offerings. "When you come into the land that I give you and reap its harvest, you shall bring the sheaf of the firstfruits of your harvest to the priest" (Leviticus 23:10)…"and the priest shall wave them with the bread of the firstfruits as a wave offering before the Lord, with the two lambs. They shall be holy to the Lord for the priest" (Leviticus 23:20).

> **FIRSTFRUITS GIVING WAS TO BE A HABIT OF ONE'S HOLY WALK WITH GOD.**

Centuries later, as Nehemiah completed the rebuilding of Jerusalem's protective wall, revived worship included firstfruit offerings — "We obligate ourselves to bring the firstfruits of our ground and the firstfruits of every tree, year by year, to the house of the Lord" (Nehemiah 10:35).

Firstfruits giving was to be a habit of holiness.

It only makes sense to presume that Solomon had this stewardship principle in mind when he offered this wisdom to his sons and daughters:

> *Proverbs 3:9-10*   Honor the Lord with your wealth and with the firstfruits of all your produce; then your barns will be filled with plenty, and your vats will be bursting with wine.

Jesus' himself echoed a similar promise as recorded by Luke.

> *Luke 6:38*   Give, and it will be given to you. Good measure, pressed down, shaken together, running over, will be put into your lap. For with the measure you use it will be measured back to you."

Being a First Fruits Steward

In his helpful volume *Money, Possessions, and Eternity*, Randy Alcorn notes what the worshipper was saying through firstfruits giving.

> "The giving of firstfruits made an important statement: 'We give our first and best to you, Lord, because we recognize our responsibility to sustain the spiritual relationship provided for us'…[It] also said, 'We trust you, God, to help us harvest the rest.' The nature of firstfruits requires it be 'taken off the top.' It's both the best and the first. As soon as it's harvested or received, it's to be given to the Lord. It's not to be stored up, hidden, hoarded, or distributed in any other way. Those who kept the best and gave God the leftovers brought God's

judgment on Israel. Giving back to the Lord, what was rightfully his, was a thermometer of faith."

One can imagine a rural shepherd surveying the scores of newborn lambs grazing on the hillside with the larger flock. One particular animal catches his eye, perfect in form, brilliant white, the very best of the birthing season. Another comes into view, alive but sickly, its gait hampered by a limp. Its birthing left some deformity, its value surely less in the marketplace. Shabbat, and worship, are but days away. "Which of these shall I bring to the Lord?" he wonders.

But there is no second guessing. He knows how good God has been to him, his family, his livelihood. "Jehovah has kept all his promises, and more, to me." The words are spoken with conviction as he moves toward the firstborn lamb. "The first," he says, "and the best," as he cradles the animal in his arms.

REFLECTION AND DISCUSSION QUESTIONS

Do you find the truth that God considers his children a kind of "firstfruits" within the larger spectrum of the human race encouraging? Clothed in the righteousness of His Son, with the Spirit flowing through us, what do you think God expects from we who are, in some sense, "the first and the best"?

What are the heart challenges that accompany whether or not to give the Lord the first and the best?

How does a commitment to firstfruits stewardship express the health of one's overall relationship with God?

THREE

MY TREASURE

Understanding Tithing

Old and New Testament Scriptures

Encountering an unexpected storm, two friends who enjoyed sailing were blown badly off course. Their damaged boat washed up on the shoreline of an uncharted, deserted island. Marooned with no working communication devices, one man paced back and forth worried and scared, while the other sat back sunning himself. The first man said to his friend, "Aren't you afraid we are about to die?" "No," said the second man. "I make $100,000 a week and tithe faithfully to my church every week. My pastor will find me."

From the earliest of my Christian experience, I've understood that God was always to get His ten cents on a dollar. When my wife taught our kids to work by delivering newspapers every day, they also learned from her that the Lord deserved the first dollars from their Tribune paycheck—at least 10% off the top.

But as is true of many things we've concluded that Scripture teaches and God expects, we may not have this whole tithing thing correct. Clarifying questions should be addressed. What did God expect of Israel according to the Law when it came to worshipping and giving?

Did "tithing" mean 10%? Was there more to it than a simple percentage? And what about today, in the New Testament or "Christian" era? How do we apply Old Testament principles and Jewish laws in our walk with Jesus? Should we? And what do the New Testament letters teach the church?

Tithing in the Old Testament Era

In a most helpful chapter, "Money and the Love of God" (in *Balancing the Christian Life,* Moody Press, 1994), Charles Ryrie offers a clear understanding of what was required in the Old Testament giving practice.

> No hard and fast rule concerning the amount [to give] is to be found among New Testament principles of giving. This is in sharp contrast to the regulations of the Old Testament, which required that a tenth of all be given to the Levites (Leviticus 27:30-33), who in turn tithed what they received and gave it to the priests.
>
> In addition, Jews understood that a second tithe (a tenth of the remaining nine-tenths) was to be set apart and consumed in a sacred meal in Jerusalem (Deuteronomy 12:5-6,11,18; those living too far from Jerusalem could bring money). Every third year, this second tithe was taken for the Levites, strangers, fatherless, and widows (Deuteronomy 14:28-29). Thus the proportion was clearly specified, and every Israelite was obliged to bring to the Lord 19% of his yearly income (p.89).

Nineteen percent, annually. Wow! And that was the *requirement.* Beyond this bottom line, there were other kinds of offerings proscribed by the Law, called "votive" (or voluntary, free-will) offerings and sacrifices. These were given when a special vow was made to the Lord. A "thank offering" was given to express special gratitude to the Lord for a blessing received.

Randy Alcorn adds, "The tithe was explicit and objective. Though God desired his people to do it joyfully, it required no heart response. But the freewill offering was entirely different. It involved the joy of a heart touched by God's grace" (*Money, Possessions, and Eternity,* Eternal Perspective Ministries, 2003).

Importantly, however, Ryrie notes "It is apparent that the tithe was part of the Mosaic Law (Lev. 27:30-33) and an important factor in the economy of Israel. [Yet] The Law was never given to the Gentiles and is expressly done away with for the Christian (Romans 2:14, 2 Corinthians 3:7-13, Hebrews 7:11-12). Neither are the words of Malachi 3 for the

Christian, for what believer claims to be a son of Jacob to whom this passage is addressed?" (p.91).

Stewardship in the New Testament Era

If we feel set a bit adrift, untethered from the Law's demands to tithe, can we nonetheless find clarity on giving from the Gospels and in letters written to Christians gathered in churches? The answer, of course, is "yes!" But it will require a bit of growing up. The stewardship teaching in the New Testament books urges generosity, the extent of which is to be determined by partnering with the Holy Spirit's prompting.

> THE O.T. LAW DEMANDED A SERIES OF TITHES, AND EXTRA VOLUNTARY OFFERINGS. THE NEW TESTAMENT URGES SOMETHING BETTER: OPEN-HANDED GENEROSITY.

In other words, we are *set free from the Law unto the freedom of the Spirit.* Set free, indeed, to do more, to be even more eagerly generous in seeking first the Kingdom of God with all that we are and have.

In *Paul and Money,* Verlyn Verbrugge and Keith Krell provide a helpful synopsis of the Apostle's instruction to Christians he was discipling.

> ...Paul places significant emphasis on the freedom of individual giving [in teaching found in 1 Corinthians 16:1-2]. He will do so again in 2 Corinthians 9:7: "Each of you should give what you have decided in your heart to give, not reluctantly or under compulsion, for God loves a cheerful giver" (NIV). Cheerful giving is voluntary giving—giving because one wants to give. This theme is also in keeping with the word "generosity" (ἁπλότης, *haplotēs*) that occurs in 2 Corinthians 8:2, 9:11,13. By its very nature, generosity is something that comes from the inside, not from outer compulsion (that certainly was the case for the Macedonians, whose spirit of generosity was so strong that they begged Paul to receive more of their income for his collection.
>
> [Craig] Bloomberg's summary for the apostolic age is pertinent here: When one turns to Acts through Revelation...one looks in vain for a reference anywhere to the tithe for believers. Indeed a more detailed scrutiny of 1 Corinthians 16:1-4 and 2 Corinthians 8-9 suggests that if all Christians gave one identical fixed percentage of their income, this would actually violate Paul's mandates. Some would be giving sacrificially, some generously, some ordinarily, and

other stingily!" (Christians in an Age of Wealth: A Biblical Theology of Stewardship, Zondervan, 2013, 129-130).

A Growing Stewardship Life

Perhaps a summary is in order. Randy Alcorn fittingly calls the practice of tithing "the training wheels of giving" (cf. Chapter 12 of *Money, Possessions, and Eternity*). His chapter provides a complete overview of Old Testament stewardship law and worship practice. "Tithing," he writes, "gives perspective. It reminds us that all we are and all we have is from God. Tithing begins as a duty but can become a delight, leading to joyful voluntary giving."

As disciples of the Lord Jesus in this era, with the Spirit of God flowing through us (John 7:37-39), we are called to more than satisfying a regulation. Paul urged that the Corinthians' giving be regular, intentional and prepared, and in keeping with how God has prospered (1 Cor. 16:1-2). To the same believers, he added it should be joyful, responsive, abundant and generous (2 Corinthians 8-9).

This means that individual believers, couples, and families should have the courage to discuss this question — "What are we giving? Why are we giving it? How are we giving it?" They should make some prayerful decisions with the New Testament open and their hearts tuned to the Holy Spirit...and then follow through.

"The point is this," Paul wrote, "whoever sows sparingly will also reap sparingly, and whoever sows bountifully will also reap bountifully. Each one must give as he has decided in his heart, not reluctantly or under compulsion, for God loves a cheerful giver" (2 Cor. 9:6-7, ESV).

REFLECTION AND DISCUSSION QUESTIONS

What insights have I gained from this overview of Old Testament stewardship and tithing? How does it contrast with what the New Testament teaches?

How have I made my (or our) decisions to give? What have been the Biblical guidelines I've used? Have I prayed and listened to the Holy Spirit when evaluating what to invest in the Kingdom of God?

How am I processing the call to "generosity?" Am I uncomfortable or comfortable with becoming a generous giver? And how does the principle of sowing and reaping impact my thinking?

FOUR

MY TREASURE

Where is it?

MATTHEW 6:19-23

> Do not store up riches for yourselves here on earth, where moths and rust destroy, and robbers break in and steal. Instead, store up riches for yourselves in heaven, where moths and rust cannot destroy, and robbers cannot break in and steal. For your heart will always be where your riches are. The eyes are like a lamp for the body. If your eyes are sound, your whole body will be full of light; but if your eyes are no good, your body will be in darkness.
> So if the light in you is darkness, how terribly dark it will be!
>
> — Jesus Christ

Are we in the dark about where our riches should be accumulated?

Not long ago, a veteran certified financial planner—author of five money books, and a frequent contributor to scores of financial/business network shows—published a short blog for Nerdwallet, entitled "The 3 Biggest Financial Decisions You'll Ever Make" (Liz Weston, March 6, 2018).

The title, of course, piques curiosity. Her picks were these three decisions.

#1 **How much education you get.** If you don't finish high school, your median net worth will drop by 44% over 2-3 decades. Even with a high school diploma, a drop of 36%. Should someone complete a two- or four-year degree, it will rise 3%. But those who complete a graduate or professional degree (especially a carefully chosen one), it soars 45% to an average of almost $700,000.

#2 **Whether you marry (and stay married).** Married couples have roughly four times the wealth of households headed by single people. And, quite candidly, divorce almost always destroys one's wealth.

#3 **Whether you own a home.** The wealth gap between homeowners and renters is enormous. Compared in one year, the median net worth of our nation's homeowners hovered around $195,000. For those satisfied to stay renters, $5,400. Owning a home and paying a mortgage is simply a solid way to be forced to save.

Sound advice, to be sure. The kind of data to inform planning and decisions shaped by wisdom. But there's something missing. Did you pick up on it?

This kind of strategizing focuses on the accumulation of net worth and wealth *here*. It answers the question, "How can I get and be rich in the 75-80 years I'm breathing on this planet?" It assumes, tragically, that *this* (i.e., our present life on this present earth) is all that there is, and all that needs to be underwritten. It advises that my riches be stored up "here," to be spent in a fleeting life that Scripture describes as "a mist that appears for a little time and then vanishes" (James 4:14). Indeed, James adds, "The sun rises with its scorching heat and withers the grass; its flower falls and its beauty perishes. So also will the rich man fade away in the midst of his pursuits" (1:11).

How could such a seasoned advisor not include in her top 3 decisions one that urged the lamplight of Jesus' Sermon on the Mount?

Our Eyes the Lamp of our Life

Let's not disparage wise planning, hard work, and good decision making for the years of life God grants us here. But the Lord Jesus and the broader testimony of Scripture are quite clear: accumulating riches and treasure only for here is a stunningly foolish approach. Unless our eyes are "sound" (Jesus' descriptor) to understand how truly short-sighted that is — unless our ears can hear the counter-cultural challenge our Lord declares — there will be a day when we are found bankrupt. We will have accumulated nothing for an existence in eternity, and all that we did accumulate is utterly gone. Naked we arrived in the world, and naked we left. We placed our treasure only where moths and rust destroy, and thieves break in and steal.

Without pointing fingers, let's have the courage to admit that we've often had "eyes" about this which Jesus suggests are "no good." Our body (his metaphor for the way we live and decide in our daily lives) has operated in the dark. Even those who truly love God, and are deeply thankful for the saving grace found in Christ, nonetheless find themselves spending the vast majority of their financial resources on temporary things, and storing up "riches for themselves here on earth."

Quite frankly, Jesus didn't sugar coat his disdain for the "store-it-up here" way of planning. When someone requested Jesus to use his influence to leverage a brother to share a family inheritance, a surprising warning coupled with a parable was the reply.

> Luke 12:14-21   But he said to him, "Man, who made me a judge or arbitrator over you?" And he said to them, "Take care, and be on your guard against all covetousness, for one's life does not consist in the abundance of his possessions."
>
> And he told them a parable, saying, "The land of a rich man produced plentifully, and he thought to himself, 'What shall I do, for I have nowhere to store my crops?' And he said, 'I will do this: I will tear down my barns and build larger ones, and there I will store all my grain and my goods. And I will say to my soul, Soul, you have ample goods laid up for many years; relax, eat, drink, be merry.' But God said to him, 'Fool! This night your soul is required of you, and the things you have prepared, whose will they be?' So is the one who lays up treasure for himself and is not rich toward God."

VERY FEW SECOND GUESS A PHILOSOPHY OF "RELAX, EAT, DRINK, AND BE MERRY. IT'S THE MOTTO OF THE AMERICAN DREAM.

Who in our money-obsessed culture would dare call this rich man a fool? More likely, he'd be commended as shrewd, regarded as savvy, invited to sit on any number of prestigious boards. Very few would second-guess his plan to "relax, eat, drink, be merry." It's the motto of the American dream.

Jesus said he was a fool. Think about that. This rich man was not aware, or perhaps had forgotten, that at any given moment, God (who holds each man's breath each moment in His hands) had decided to "require his soul" of him. He suddenly died.

The moment of accountability had come, and he would stand before the One who had endowed him with a stewardship — ability and resources. But now, he appear before the Throne a pauper, having stored up treasure for himself, neglecting becoming rich toward God.

Jesus' Positive Encouragement

About so many things, Mother Teresa had good eyes. "Anything that is not given," she once remarked, "is lost."

Our Lord affirms his eagerness for us to "store up for yourselves riches in heaven, where moths and rust cannot destroy and robbers cannot break in and steal." What could have the rich landowner and family done with his extra crops and mushrooming stockpile of goods? It appears Jesus expects that he would have recognized the blessing hand of God upon his life (instead of merely his own successful productivity), and embraced the role of a steward of endowed resources.

Later in Luke 12, the Lord speaks about a "faithful and wise manager" who is doing what his Master desires with what has been put in his trust (in this life). Such a manager will be given the joy of greater responsibility when the Master returns (12:41-44).

Our heart focuses its affection and energy on where we have placed our treasure. When as stewards we invest the treasure — the resources God has placed in our hands — in matters which advance the gospel and the kingdom of God, we have assurance of being rich toward God. With eyes full of this light, our walk before God shines.

REFLECTION AND DISCUSSION QUESTIONS

Why do we often assume that those who can make and accumulate money are wise, even admirable?

What makes it difficult to give away when we have extra? How does the desire to feel secure and safe play into our thinking? What about trusting in Someone we can't see vs. trusting in resources that we can?

Am I making specific decisions, and taking radically generous steps, in order to store up riches in heaven? What do I hear the Word of God and the Spirit of God saying to me (us) about this?

FIVE

MY TREASURE

Which is it?

Matthew 6:24   "No one can serve two masters, for either he will hate the one and love the other, or he will be devoted to the one and despise the other. You cannot serve God and money."

1 Timothy 6:9-10   "But those who desire to be rich fall into temptation, into a snare, into many senseless and harmful desires that plunge people into ruin and destruction. For the love of money is a root of all kinds of evils. It is through this craving that some have wandered away from the faith and pierced themselves with many pangs."

For a dozen seasons or more, the popularity of ABC television's "Shark Tank" has steadily grown. Americans by the millions watch the lively bargain-n-business banter religiously. Each episode features a group of aggressive, shrewd entrepreneurs who — already proven in money-making skill — interview those with fledging business ideas or novel products, products which have (or so argue the presenters) the potential of making even more dollars by the millions.

The panel of "sharks" (usually 5 in the room) are both eager and tough minded. They ask hard what's-in-it-for-me questions. When the business venture shows merit, they compete with each other for the opportunity to partner and invest. Their sole objective in agreeing to invest, coach, and open doors to greater market share is quite clear. As one shark (Kevin O'Leary, self-designated as "Mr. Wonderful") regularly reminds everyone: "I LOVE money!!"

Who doesn't? But what is money, and why do we learn to love it?

Money is an agreed upon economic medium (e.g., coins, official paper bills with numerical designation, etc.) which facilitates for people the exchange of things needed to live or desired to experience. We all understand that different items have varying values, values established by the factors of supply (i.e., how much of it is available) and demand (how eager are people to obtain it).

In any given society, its members assess both what they need to live and how much it costs (either in terms of working so as to personally secure it, or the amount of money required to pay). We also learn through experience that having more money allows us to obtain more things, things which last or retain their value longer over time. People who accumulate wealth usually have a very different lifestyle than those who live on little. They also, typically, are afforded more respect, sometimes are offered more privileges and opportunities than those who have much less money. As the saying goes, "The rich get richer and the poor get poorer."

Let's not forget that those who live in well-developed countries have so much more than others in the rest of the world. If you live in Australia, for example, the average annual income is around $55,000; should you dwell in Honduras you have about $2,150 to live on each year. In Madagascar, $400. In Russia, about $9,720; in the United States, $56,000.

What Are We To Love?

So it is normal, even cultural, and desirable to get and be rich. Yet in becoming a disciple of the Lord Jesus Christ, is there a radical transformation called for by our Master?

It seems so. Jesus' statement found in Matthew 6:24 could hardly address more clearly the struggle. "No one," he insisted, "can serve two masters." Money will either be loved or hated. If money is loved, God will be hated. If God is loved, money will be despised. Despised, it seems, because of its potential to capture our hearts, replacing dollar signs on the seat of the throne belonging to God alone. The Lord's statement urges us to evaluate: Do I love God or do I love money? Will I serve God or will I serve money? What, or Who, is my true treasure? The answer will identify the location of my heart.

Randy Alcorn (*Money, Possessions, and Eternity*) articulates the questions pertinent to our affluent experience:

> What is your treasure? Is it your house? car? boat? library? gun-collection? Is your treasure in art, coins, or gold? Is it in savings, a retirement program, insurance policies, annuities, real estate, or commodities? Is your treasure 500 shares of AT&T or Microsoft? Some people may own these items without them necessarily being their treasure. *But every possession we hold onto presents a constant temptation that it will become our treasure.*

Money Is Not Evil, But Can Be...Or Not

Paul's warning through Timothy to Christians under his teaching ministry is timely and insightful (1 Timothy 6:9-10). If one's principal objective in life (and please, let's be honest with ourselves should we think, "That's not me!") is to *be rich*, we are traveling down an oft unrecognized yet thoroughly dangerous pathway. We will likely be snared (i.e., caught and captured) chasing wealth, and the satisfaction it gives our "flesh."

> **LOVING MONEY IS AN EVIL ROOT FROM WHICH SPRINGS MUCH EVIL. CONVERSELY, ONE'S PRIMARY PASSION FOR GOD CAN BE FANNED INTO GODLY GENEROSITY.**

What's more, there's every possibility of being plunged into senseless and harmful desires. Subtly and profoundly our lives are being ruined, destroyed. Worse, an insatiable craving for more money both fails to truly satisfy at the same time it misleads. We wander off from God. The hot coals of once fervent faith in God become gray, cold ashes.

Loving money is the *root* of all kinds of *evil*. From this love grows sinful fruit. The term Paul uses for evil, *kakon*, points to that which destroys one's sense of morality, a confusion about (if not a redefinition of) what is right and what is wrong. In other words, loving money (and all that one might do or experience with lots of it) can make doing what is wrong permissible, while neglecting to do what is good not really a problem. It messes with God's righteousness.

On the other hand, one's primary passion for God can be fanned into flame through the generous use of assets and money. Who better illustrates this than the son of encouragement, Barnabas? A new Christian, perhaps from a family with resources, he "sells a field that belongs to him and brought the money and laid it at the apostles' feet" (Acts 4:32, for distribution among the needy in the early church).

Conversely (Acts 5:1-10), it is not inconceivable that Ananias and Saphira were snared by their love of money, convincing them it was acceptable to be deceptive about their giving to the church. The ruin it brought upon their own lives sobered the young church significantly (Acts 5:11).

Once Again, Storing It Above And Beyond

What we can do is love God with the way we use the money he entrusts to us. Paul's additional word through Timothy provides a positive pathway.

> *1 Timothy 6:17-19* As for the rich in this present age, charge them not to be haughty, nor to set their hopes on the uncertainty of riches, but on God, who richly provides us with everything to enjoy. They are to do good, to be rich in good works, to be generous and ready to share, thus storing up treasure for themselves as a good foundation for the future, so that they may take hold of that which is truly life.

Endowed with more, our hearts must be wisely vigilant. Money should humble us, not inflate our pride. Money should awaken us to opportunity for kingdom-advancing ministry rather than become our security in a life that is unchangeably temporary. With hopes set on God, and on God alone, we are free to enjoy what He provides without being entrapped in indulgence.

Paul echoes what we discovered previously (cf. Matthew 6:9-13, Luke 12:13-21). We can store up treasure above, a foundation for life in eternity. Since God is being truthful with us in this, what we "store above" will truly make a difference in the experience of life in eternity. And, in so doing — in making specific discipleship choices about how we handle and use money — we take hold today of life the way our wonderful Lord intended.

REFLECTION AND DISCUSSION QUESTIONS

How were you taught the importance and value of money? When you became a disciple of Jesus, did you need to unlearn anything that you had been taught or seen modeled for you?

What are some of the best examples you've seen of someone who loved God first (and solely) in using his/her financial resources for the kingdom?

Is there an insight from this chapter that struck an important chord in your thinking? If so, what difference will that make in how you view and use money going forward?

SIX

MY TREASURE

God's Priorities and Promises

Matthew 6:25-33, Philippians 4:10-20

Matthew 6:25-33 "Therefore I tell you, do not be anxious about your life, what you will eat or what you will drink, nor about your body, what you will put on. Is not life more than food, and the body more than clothing? Look at the birds of the air: they neither sow nor reap nor gather into barns, and yet your heavenly Father feeds them. Are you not of more value than they? And which of you by being anxious can add a single hour to his span of life? And why are you anxious about clothing? Consider the lilies of the field, how they grow: they neither toil nor spin, yet I tell you, even Solomon in all his glory was not arrayed like one of these.

 But if God so clothes the grass of the field, which today is alive and tomorrow is thrown into the oven, will he not much more clothe you, O you of little faith?

 Therefore do not be anxious, saying, 'What shall we eat?' or 'What shall we drink?' or 'What shall we wear?' For the Gentiles seek after all these things, and your heavenly Father knows that you need them all. But seek first the kingdom of God and his righteousness, and all these things will be added to you.

Who hasn't read these words from the lips of Jesus of Nazareth and (at least inside) said, "Yeah, right"? For many, deep seated doubt is the initial reaction. While not wanting to be disrespectful, we are not overly anxious to simply "go there" and live as Jesus is teaching.

Truth is that we've spent most of our lives worrying or at least thinking A LOT about the food we consume and the clothing hanging around our frames. "What are we going to have for supper? Really? I don't really care for that. Can't we have something else? Ah...c'mon!"

Some often worry, if not obsess, over what to wear. Is it in style? Is it cool? Does it fit the occasion, the event? Will others size me up by what I've chosen to put on? What does my clothing say about me? We get tired of the same shirt, last year's dress. If fashion suddenly shifts direction showing models on runways with torn jeans or knee-high boots, we've got to figure out how to get a pair...or three!

And, unfortunately for us, easy credit often encourages unwise purchasing of more than what God has already amply provided.

Anxious in Worry or Confident in Faith

Jesus repeats the word "anxious." It can be translated "worry," a Greek verb meaning "to be drawn in different directions, even distracted." When we worry about something, it becomes the elephant-in-the-room of our minds, a default in thinking. There's an unresolved conflict between our desire for something and the prospect that we will, in fact, obtain it. Such a nurtured desire begins to dominate our attention. We plan and act to have our perceived need met *the way we want it to be met.* Other things — usually more important things — are not attended to. Our focus becomes what our flesh craves (i.e., food) or what our pride longs for (i.e., beautiful clothing).

But then walking with Jesus, we hear him say, "Will you let some of that go? You have, don't you know, a Father who feeds worry-free birds, a Provider who clothes fields with brilliantly colorful flowers. Why are you distracted from what is truly important by these already provided things?"

Our Lord challenges what WE have concluded to be important. He seeks to replace it with real food and trusting faith.

This was so very clear when Jesus took his disciples through

Samaria (John 4). You'll remember that at the well outside of town, Jesus encountered a very needy woman, trying to find satisfaction in water from Jacob's well rather than what was available in the Messiah's gift.

At mid-day it was the usual time to find lunch, which is exactly what his disciples ran off to do. But when they returned with food in hand, they were stunned not only to see Jesus talking with this woman, but also checked up when he said (in essence) "I've already eaten the food I need." He was speaking of food His Father had given him in spending time helping reclaim a women from a misspent live. Jesus went on to say that their attention would be better spent lifting up their eyes from food-in-hand and taking in the opportunity for harvesting.

> **OUR LORD DESIRES TO RESHAPE OUR VALUES PARADIGM. FAITHLESS PURSUITS SHOULD END. GENUINE TRUST OUGHT BEGIN.**

Our Lord's reshaping of our value system not only calls for stopping something — choosing NOT to worry about food and clothing — but also for starting something much more important.

On the one hand, to stop living like those who place the most value on things (i.e., Gentiles, those who do not know God nor have a faith family-based confidence in Him). "For the Gentiles seek after all these things." We need not lemming-like join in their anxiousness-driven pursuit. "You have a Father who knows you need these things."

On the other hand, start living like those who place value and attention on the things of God's kingdom, and on living out His (endowed) righteousness. "Seek first..." is a clarion call. If you are going to be, in the right sense, anxious about anything, be anxious over the things God deems crucial. The advance of His kingdom. The expression of His righteousness. And to that, we could add all kinds of important kingdom initiatives. How about your lost neighbor's salvation? How about the discipleship growth of young Christians in your local church? How about that young couple that needs some marriage mentoring? How about that called missionary who needs additional monthly support, or the orphans housed at a faith-based orphanage? How about the need of so many in the world who have not yet heard the name of Christ or the gospel?

How about that woman-at-the-well you know?

The Promise Attending the Priority

"And all these things (adequate food and clothing) will be added to you." What a promise!

Paul made the same promise to the young Christians in the Philippian church. "And my God will supply every need of yours according to his riches in glory in Christ Jesus (Philippians 4:19)." What a promise! But it is based on a "putting first" which the Christians in that church had done.

> *Philippians 4:14-18* Yet it was kind of you to share my trouble. And you Philippians yourselves know that in the beginning of the gospel, when I left Macedonia, no church entered into partnership with me in giving and receiving, except you only. Even in Thessalonica you sent me help for my needs once and again. Not that I seek the gift, but I seek the fruit that increases to your credit. I have received full payment, and more. I am well supplied, having received from Epaphroditus the gifts you sent, a fragrant offering, a sacrifice acceptable and pleasing to God.

Here a church faithful to providing for Paul's needs in ministry time and time again, a putting-first of the Kingdom of God and his righteousness. Consequently, Paul's assuring word that God would be faithful to supply "every need" from the vast storehouse of His riches in glory in Christ. Quite a treasure from which to draw indeed.

REFLECTION AND DISCUSSION QUESTIONS

The Bible reminds us that our trust (or faith) in God — that He will be good on His promises to us — is what thoroughly pleases Him (Hebrews 11:6). Why do we find it so difficult at times to trust Him to provide what we genuinely need?

It seems clear that some of us are more prone to worry than others. Do you think the anxious-prone are granted an exemption from the command to set aside worry?

When you have put God first, has He ever failed to meet a true need in your life? How can this reality provide future confidence in your walk with God?

SEVEN

MY TREASURE

Faithfully Generous

Mark 12:41-44, 2 Corinthians 8-9

I don't know what it's like with you, but I do know what it's like with me when money gets tight. I get nervous and cranky. And usually in that order.

First, I get nervous. Dictionary.com illustrates "cranky" with "I'm always cranky when I don't get enough sleep." Yep, that's me. When money is tight, I become apprehensive. I'm not sure how I'm going to meet all the obligations that I've committed to, that are staring me in the face, without incurring some debt. There have been plenty of nights over the decades of our marriage when I lay awake at night wondering how I was going to provide for my family, to pay for that unexpected car repair, or to have enough money just to get home close to family for the holidays. Over the years, I've been nervous a lot.

Which leads to getting cranky. Again, the dictionary says being cranky is "ill-tempered, grouchy, cross." The sentence dictionary.com used to illustrate the word was I'm always cranky when I don't get enough sleep. I modified that. I'm always cranky when money is tight. Many a night I've poured over the checkbook, looking at receipts, and irritated at the way I had spent some money, or my wife had spent some money. Frustrated that we weren't more wise. "Really, another pair of shoes?" Of course, my expenditures always made a lot more sense than hers... right guys?

Tight money leads to nervous crankiness...and nervous crankiness over tight $ can lead to compromise. In our home, we've always had a commitment to giving first to the Lord, at least 10%, and usually more than that. But....but when money gets tight, how easy it has been for me to nervously and crankily say, "Well, Lord...I'm going to put you on hold for a few weeks or so...so I can get myself out of this mess. I'm sorry, God...$$ is too tight; I'm too nervous; I've got to compromise on what really belongs to you."

And, we figure, "Well, if I just had a lot of money, I could really be generous with God, and really generous with others. Even my family. I'm just a lot of money away from being a really generous person."

Is that how God defines generosity...that only really wealthy people can afford to be generous?

May we explore a stunning encounter that Jesus and his men had one afternoon in the middle of a busy day? Mark records the encounter (Mark 4:41-44). Here's the context:
- This encounter happens in Jerusalem, Israel's ancient capital and holy city
- This encounter happens after Jesus has entered the city in a triumphal way and the people have been praising God for his coming and wondering if He really is God's Messiah...which is causing all kinds of consternation with the religious leadership of the nation
- This encounter happens in the temple area — the power center for all these religious leaders
  - ✓ the place where the worship of the nation happens,
  - ✓ the place that Jesus cleaned out just a few days earlier because of all the financial corruption going on with the exorbitant prices merchants were charging for sacrificial animals and the rates of exchange of Roman coinage for Jewish coinage
  - ✓ the place where Jesus began openly teaching all the people coming to worship, and being challenged by the Sadducees and the Scribes and the Priests and the Jewish Elders

In other words, this all happens in the temple where God's soon to be crucified Son, Jesus, is cleaning out the corruption and being challenged each step of the way. In fact, Jesus doesn't pull any punches about the corruption of the leaders running the temple.

And in his teaching he said, "Beware of the scribes, who like to walk around in long robes and like greetings in the marketplaces and have the best seats in the synagogues and the places of honor at feasts, who devour widows' houses and for a pretense make long prayers. They will receive the greater condemnation" (Mark 12:38-39).

Jesus was no friend to all the prideful shenanigans being pulled off by these religious leaders in the temple. Rather, he called it out. "They strut around like they are big spiritual stuff," Jesus said, "but all they are really doing is devouring the little income that widows have."

> *Mark 12:41-42* And he sat down opposite the treasury and watched the people putting money into the offering box. Many rich people put in large sums. And a poor widow came and put in two small copper coins, which make a penny.
>
> [Jesus sat down..] on a bench to watch the people bring in their contributions to the temple treasury. According to the Mishnah, Shekalim VI.5, there were 13 trumpet shaped receptacles—wide at the top, narrow down on the end —for this purpose placed against the wall of the Court of the Women. (William Lane, *The Gospel of Mark*, 442.)

So...what did Jesus observe? Mark tells it simply. On the one hand, "Many rich people put in large sums." It must have been the day when the rich gathered to publicly pour in the open mouths of the trumpet receptacles "large sums." Not hard to image people bringing in bags of brass/copper coins and pouring the coins out in each of the trumpets, with all the accompanying sound. These were the wealthy people of the city, of the nation. They had it, and they gave some of it.

Suddenly in stark contrast, a poor widow stands in the same line as the others. Her demeanor, her clothing, her condition immediately recognized. What's more she came with the smallest amount of offering allowable. You could not contribute if you had any less (which suggests that perhaps she had to save even to come up with this) than two "lepta." Two of the smallest copper coins. "The tiny lepton," comments Lane, "was worth about 1/400th part of a shekel, or roughly 1/8th of a cent." So she walks up to one of the trumpet containers, flush with emptied bags of coins, and puts in a total of one-fourth of a penny. A moment later, she is gone. Who knew?

Eyes To See Genuine Generosity

That's what Jesus saw—a tremendous contrast, a contrast he insisted on pointing out to his disciples. "And he called his disciples to him... (Mark 12:43)" Why did Jesus have to do that? I take it they weren't watching. Perhaps they had not understood in the first place why they needed to sit the better part of an afternoon watching the shuffle of the offering line.

More accurate still, they probably saw the woman yet concluding she was nothing special. So Jesus had to say, "Let me tell you something. You've just seen something I've been waiting to observe all afternoon. That woman is why we are here."

> Mark 12:43-44 and said to them, "Truly, I say to you, this poor widow has put in more than all those who are contributing to the offering box. For they all contributed out of their abundance, but she out of her poverty has put in everything she had, all she had to live on."

In other words, he was telling them, "That woman is the most generous person you/I have ever met." Gentlemen! Generosity is not an amount; it is an act of faith. Generosity is never simply a matter of how much; it is always a matter of how much you trust God when you give!

Listen to Jesus' two-part explanation. First, he asserts that generosity is never simply a matter of how much. You can give a lot, and frankly, not even break a sweat. "For they all contributed out of their abundance," the Master observes (Mark 12:44a). The word Jesus uses here for "abundance" is περισσενω (*perisseuo*) meaning "that which was more than enough, that which is left over, surplus." Others gave out of their "extra." Sure, they poured a lot in, but only because they knew they still had a lot at home. They were trusting in what they had kept in reserve.

And that's OK. Jesus isn't dismissing their giving. It's just not generous. It was their abundance made them feel comfortable to give. Frankly, they wouldn't miss it. Their reserved abundance made their giving "safe." No need to trust anyone or any thing but what they have tucked away. That's why generosity is never simply a matter of how much (i.e., the amount). You can give a lot and not even break a sweat.

But secondly, here is what got Jesus' attention, why he called his disciples to open their eyes. Generous giving, true generosity, is always about how much faith. "But she out of her poverty has put in everything she had, all she had to live on" (Matthew 12:44b).

Again, William Lane deftly observes, "She had two coins, she could easily have kept one for herself." He adds, "Jesus saw in the widow an example which the disciples needed to appreciate...what the Twelve had failed to appreciate was the total commitment to God that this widow's gift represented.

The most generous person Jesus ever met — a poor widow who willingly threw in her last two coins — trusted God for whatever would be needed next in her life.

> **TRUE GENEROSITY IS NEVER ABOUT HOW MUCH, BUT ABOUT HOW MUCH FAITH.**

Generosity the Call of the New Testament

Generosity is never merely about how much; it is always about how much faith the giving represents.

This key truth finds example in the wonderful giving of the Jerusalem church (Acts 4:32-37) and continued expression frequently in letters to Christians in first century churches. Like a cheerleader, Paul trumpeted the practices found in Macedonia.

> *2 Corinthians 8:1-5* We want you to know, brothers, about the grace of God that has been given among the churches of Macedonia, for in a severe test of affliction, their abundance of joy and their extreme poverty have overflowed in a wealth of generosity on their part. For they gave according to their means, as I can testify, and beyond their means, of their own accord, begging us earnestly for the favor of taking part in the relief of the saints—and this, not as we expected, but they gave themselves first to the Lord and then by the will of God to us.

Paul urged this example to be repeated by the Christians in Corinth. "He who supplies seed to the sower and bread for food will supply and multiply your seed for sowing and increase the harvest of your righteousness. You will be enriched in every way to be generous in every way, which through us will produce thanksgiving to God (2 Corinthians 9:10-11).

Ready to be generous toward God? He will supply all you and I need to be so.

REFLECTION AND DISCUSSION QUESTIONS

What generous persons have you known in your life? What have you seen in them that exemplifies the principles found in this chapter?

Are there challenges that arise in your mind as you consider being a generous steward toward God and others? What are they? What initial steps is the Spirit of God urging you to take to become more eagerly generous?

Our ministry's value of RADICAL GENEROSITY is stated as "living adventurously to impact our world," in order to accomplish the mission of connecting people to life-defining relationships in Christ. What connections can you make between living (and giving) adventurously and connecting people to Christ? How might your generous giving make this happen?

EIGHT

MY TREASURE

The Rewards of Stewardship Investing

Luke 12:41-48, 19:11-27, Matthew 25:14-30

Luke 12:41-48 Peter said, "Lord, are you telling this parable for us or for all?"

And the Lord said, "Who then is the faithful and wise manager, whom his master will set over his household, to give them their portion of food at the proper time? Blessed is that servant whom his master will find so doing when he comes. Truly, I say to you, he will set him over all his possessions.

But if that servant says to himself, 'My master is delayed in coming,' and begins to beat the male and female servants, and to eat and drink and get drunk, the master of that servant will come on a day when he does not expect him and at an hour he does not know, and will cut him in pieces and put him with the unfaithful.

And that servant who knew his master's will but did not get ready or act according to his will, will receive a severe beating. But the one who did not know, and did what deserved a beating, will receive a light beating.

Everyone to whom much was given, of him much will be required, and from him to whom they entrusted much, they will demand the more.

The parabolic charge from Jesus to which Peter refers is in Luke 12:33-40. It falls within a broader chapter packed with important instruction for disciples:

- A warning not to allow the "leaven" of hypocrisy to permeate one's thinking and living, giving a show on the outside without genuine spiritual life on the inside (12:1-3)
- An encouragement not to fear those who stridently oppose your commitment to following Jesus (12:4-7), to be Spirit empowered in one's bold witness (12:8-12)
- A rebuke to those who lay up personal treasure but are not rich toward God (12:13-21)
- An exhortation to fully trust a providing heavenly Father for all that you need, eagerly laying up treasure above (12:22-34, cf. Matthew 6:19-34)

Then, the parable begins with "Stay dressed for action; keep your lamps burning." It's a word about daily being prepared for the Master "when he comes and knocks" at the door, so that the prepared wedding feast can begin! "Blessed are those servants whom the master finds awake (i.e., no matter in what "watch" he may arrive) when he comes... blessed are those servants" (Luke 12:36-38).

"You must be ready, for the Son of Man is coming at an hour you do not expect" (vs.40). Peter wonders, "Are you talking about just us (i.e., his disciples) or for all?"

What follows is a rather thought-provoking, if not arresting, reply from Jesus illustrating clearly his expectation of those who manage "his household."

The Master's Teaching on Stewardship

The parable we find in Luke 12:41-48 is reinforced both in Luke 19:11-27, as well as in Matthew 25:14-30. There are some common elements in all three passages.

The Lord's stories focus on a stewardship arrangement between a "master" (i.e., God) and his "servants" (i.e., people, and more specifically, disciples).

- The master owns everything, but has entrusted the management and development of his assets to his servants for a time even while he is away
- The expectation is that the servants understand the master's expectation and are responsible for the diligent use, investment,

management, and multiplication of what was entrusted
- Those servants who engage in such ongoing diligence are living in a way that is fitting with the master's anticipated return, and will be rewarded generously for such faithfulness
- Those rewards for stewardship diligence involve greater honor, authority, and responsibility in an era to come
- Those servants who neglect such diligent management of the master's assets choose to live unproductively, foolishly, unprepared for the master's return. Rather than reward, they will suffer consequences (even severe!) for such mismanagement

Admittedly, passages like these can be more than a little unsettling. Many Christians — perhaps most — have been taught in essence that nothing truly negative lies ahead for the one whose sins have been fully forgiven by the blood of Christ. Such full forgiveness, to be sure, is what God promises to every one who places faith in Christ's finished work on the cross. No child of God will suffer any of God's wrath which our sinful condition and choices deserve.

However, this solid assurance should not mute what the Spirit through Scripture also teaches about the rewarding of those disciples giving obedient faithfulness to the Master's kingdom business. The Bible is clear that the Lord will evaluate faithfulness and fruitfulness. And, some servants will be honored with reward in a future age while others will suffer the loss of commendation and reward in failing to take seriously the Master's endowment and expectation. Indeed, Jesus speaks of this rewarding vividly, the experience of great joy for faithfulness vs. the experience of significant shame.

> **THE PENALTY FOR OUR SIN HAS BEEN SATISFIED AT THE CROSS. YET IT'S CLEAR THAT THE LORD WILL EVALUATE OUR FAITHFULNESS AND FRUITFULNESS.**

The Lord's parables, recorded in the gospels, are mirrored in other apostolic teaching.

> *Romans 8:16-17* The Spirit himself bears witness with our spirit that we are children of God, and if children, then heirs—heirs of God and fellow heirs with Christ, provided we suffer with him in order that we may also be glorified with him.

1 Corinthians 3:9-15   For we are God's fellow workers. You are God's field, God's building. According to the grace of God given to me, like a skilled master builder I laid a foundation, and someone else is building upon it. Let each one take care how he builds upon it. For no one can lay a foundation other than that which is laid, which is Jesus Christ. Now if anyone builds on the foundation with gold, silver, precious stones, wood, hay, straw—each one's work will become manifest, for the Day will disclose it, because it will be revealed by fire, and the fire will test what sort of work each one has done. If the work that anyone has built on the foundation survives, he will receive a reward. If anyone's work is burned up, he will suffer loss, though he himself will be saved, but only as through fire.

2 Corinthians 5:9-10   So whether we are at home or away, we make it our aim to please him. For we must all appear before the judgment seat of Christ, so that each one may receive what is due for what he has done in the body, whether good or evil.

Colossians 3:23-24   Whatever you do, work heartily, as for the Lord and not for men, knowing that from the Lord you will receive the inheritance as your reward. You are serving the Lord Christ.

2 Timothy 2:11-13   The saying is trustworthy, for:
If we have died with him, we will also live with him;
if we endure, we will also reign with him;
if we deny him, he also will deny us;
if we are faithless, he remains faithful—

2 Timothy 4:6-8   For I am already being poured out as a drink offering, and the time of my departure has come. I have fought the good fight, I have finished the race, I have kept the faith. Henceforth there is laid up for me the crown of righteousness, which the Lord, the righteous judge, will award to me on that day, and not only to me but also to all who have loved his appearing.

James 1:12   Blessed is the man who remains steadfast under trial, for when he has stood the test he will receive the crown of life, which God has promised to those who love him.

2 John 1:7-8   For many deceivers have gone out into the world, those who do not confess the coming of Jesus Christ in the flesh. Such a one is the deceiver and the antichrist. Watch yourselves, so that you may not lose what we have worked for, but may win a full reward.

These passages from the Epistles, rightly interpreted, should not be considered to be only complementary descriptions of landing in "heaven," enjoying the gift of eternal life.   More specifically, they reinforce an important, yet often overlooked reality. Namely, that while eternal life is a free gift "by grace through faith," rewards will be awarded for faithful, diligent obedience to the callings of the Master. He has endowed each of his servants with his resources. He expects (and indeed empowers through His Spirit) recognition of that endowment, and faithfulness in using them for the discipleship mission of the church (cf. Matthew 28:19-20).

In other words, how we as disciple-servants choose to use all that the Lord has put under our stewardship (strength, time, abilities and giftings, the engagement in our vocation, financial resources) will be evaluated, and can be rewarded.

Faithfulness and Rewards

Randy Alcorn (*Money, Possessions and Eternity*, Kindle Edition, p. 135) addresses what may be our internal objection regarding any expectation of being rewarded in the age to come. Should we be motivated by the prospect of reward for faithful stewardship of what God has entrusted to us? Is that OK? Alcorn affirms what Scripture encourages.

> God created us with certain desires, and he made us to be motivated by rewards that appeal to those desires.
> He calls us to act on the basis of those promised rewards. As we've seen, the Scriptures are full of exhortations to act in certain ways to gain certain rewards. Yet there persists a misguided belief that desire for power, possessions, and pleasure in the next life is crass and to pursue rewards is selfish or mercenary. Three godly Englishmen of three different centuries offer us a very different perspective, an explicitly biblical one.
> John Bunyan, the seventeenth-century pastor who was imprisoned for preaching the gospel, said of eternal rewards, "They are such as should make us leap to think on, and that we should remember with exceeding joy, and never think that it is contrary to the Christian faith, to rejoice and be glad for [them]."
> William Wilberforce, through his tireless efforts in Parliament in the early nineteenth century, finally succeeded in abolishing England's slave trade. He devoted most of his fortune to the cause of Christ. This was his perspective on our God-given desires: "Christianity proposes not to extinguish our natural desires. It promises to bring the desires under just control and direct them to their true object."
> C. S. Lewis, a professor at Oxford and Cambridge in the mid-twentieth century, wrote prolifically on the Christian faith. He diverted most of his royalties to charitable causes and individual needs, living simply and thinking often of the world:
>
>> The faint, far-off results of those energies which God's

creative rapture implanted in matter when He made the worlds are what we now call physical pleasures; and even thus filtered, they are too much for our present management. What would it be to taste at the fountainhead that stream of which even these lower reaches prove so intoxicating? Yet that, I believe, is what lies before us. The whole man is to drink joy from the fountain of joy.

The New Testament has a lot to say about self-denial, but not about self-denial as an end in itself. We are told to deny ourselves and to take up our cross in order to follow Christ—and nearly every description of what we shall ultimately find if we do so contains an appeal to desire. If there lurks in most modern minds the notion that it's a bad thing to desire one's own good and earnestly hope for enjoyment, it is because it has crept in from the teachings of Immanuel Kant and the ancient Stoics. Certainly, it has no part in the Christian faith.

Indeed, if we consider the unblushing promises of rewards promised in the Gospels, it would seem that our Lord finds our desires not too strong, but too weak. We are half-hearted creatures, fooling about with drink and sex and ambition when infinite joy has been offered to us. We are far too easily pleased, like an ignorant child who goes on making mud pies in a slum because he cannot imagine what is meant by an offer of a holiday at the sea.

Heeding The Master's Call

Alcorn quotes Puritan pastor Richard Baxter, who asked this probing question (in 1649):

If there be so certain and glorious a rest for the saints, why is there no more industrious seeking after it? One would think, if a man did once hear of such unspeakable glory to be obtained, and believed what he heard to be true, he should be transported with the vehemency of his desire after it, and should almost forget to eat and drink, and should care for nothing else, and speak of and inquire after nothing else, but how to get this treasure. And yet people who hear of it daily, and profess to believe it as a fundamental article of their faith, do as little mind it, or labour for it, as if they had never heard of any such thing, or did not believe one word they hear.

He adds, "May we joyously believe. And then may we live as if we believe!" [*Money, Possessions, and Eternity*, Kindle Edition. p.138.]

REFLECTION AND DISCUSSION QUESTIONS

What new discoveries about your stewardship did you make in personally processing this chapter? What surprised you? What questions does it raise?

Understanding that a future age will be the time when disciple-servants will be awarded for faithfulness, how does it deepen or expand your view of what's ahead for Christians?

Are you clear about the difference between God's giving us eternal life (freely by faith) and God challenging us to earn reward for faithfulness? Could you explain this to someone else? Which passages of Scripture would you use to demonstrate the difference?

NINE

MY TREASURE

The Quicksand of Debt

ROMANS 13:8
Owe no one anything, except to love each other,
for the one who loves another has fulfilled the law.

There's little denying we live in a world-wide culture of comfort with indebtedness. Extraordinary indebtedness. Our United States government is well over $20 trillion in debt, quickly trending toward $30 trillion — an amount defying imagination. U.S. consumer debt exceeds $4 trillion. On average (as this is being written) each American carries over $90,000 in personal debt.

Conversely, according to research published in 2020, only 22% of Americans have $1000-$5000 in savings, one-third have less than $1000, and 40% of Americans do not have enough money on hand to cover a $400 emergency.

In the USA, both the government of the people and the people under the government are debtors.

Perhaps what Scripture says to Christians comes as a smelling-salts surprise. "Owe no one anything." Paul's command in Romans 13 echoes other Scriptural injunctions which warn of the enslavement brought on by being in debt.

What Is Debt?

Dr. Charles Ryrie points out that in the Greek text of Romans 13:8 one finds a double negative, used by Paul (and the Holy Spirit) for emphasis. In other words, there is no way that disciples of Jesus Christ should have any outstanding debts except, God says, "the debt of love, which even though it is paid every day can never be fully paid" (Charles Ryrie, "Owe a man? Oh no, man!" *Moody Magazine,* March 1979).

Admittedly, even Christians who fully honor and seek to obey Scripture disagree over what it means to be "in debt." Many questions fuel honest discussion. What does it mean "to owe"? Does Scripture actually require immediate, cash-in-full transactions? Is utilizing temporary or short-term debt permissible? Is there "good debt" vs. "bad debt"? Is carrying debt on an appreciating item (e.g., a home mortgage or other likely, accruing-in-value item like quality art-work or real estate) acceptable?

Ryrie explains that "if liabilities exceed assets, then a family is in debt. A family whose annual budget shows a deficit is in serious trouble." He recognizes that monthly balance sheets may be in the red or in the black if income is received irregularly or in larger chunks. "But income must be greater in other months to compensate over a twelve-month period." In other words, to be consistently "in the red" over time is what Scripture prohibits; that is, "unbiblical" debt.

Old Testament Loan and Debt Practices

Quite frankly, debt is nothing to toy with. The Bible repeatedly warns how unwise and enslaving indebtedness is, and the Old Testament Law contained provisions preventing harsh treatment when money was loaned and repaid.

Indeed loans were permitted, both to fellow Jewish countrymen (Lev. 25:35-38, yet only without interest) and to foreigners (Deut.23:20, permission to charge interest). Yet any unkind, exacting management of loaned money was out of bounds (cf. Exodus 22:25-27). Collateral for a loan could not include keeping a poor man's garment overnight (Ex. 22:26-27). A widow's garment was not to be taken in pledge (Deut. 24:17). Furthermore, a person's means of livelihood could not be put in jeopardy in the negotiating of the terms of a loan (Deut. 24:6). Nor was anyone permitted to forcibly enter someone's home to collect what might be owed (Deut. 24:10-13).

Found in the priestly code are the provisions of Leviticus 25, those of the Year of Jubilee. Every 50th year, the land given to God's people was given a gracious, year-long Sabbath rest. The asset of land could not be sold in perpetuity to another. Rather, it was to be returned to the original family after use for crop-raising and debt settling. The option to redeem such land was to be honored. Homes sold could be reclaimed.

And, included in Jubilee law were directions for settling long-standing debts in a reasonable fashion. Usury (i.e., charging excessive interest) was strictly forbidden.

The spirit of these provisions encouraged God's people to treat each other in financial matters with grace and generosity. They were not to take advantage of one another, so that none would be permanently imprisoned in debt.

When the Law was given through Moses a second time, it included a further requirement for a creditor to "grant a lease" of what he has lent to his kinsman neighbor every 7th year. "He shall not exact it of his neighbor, his brother, because the Lord's release has been proclaimed" (Deut. 15:1-2), specifically for ensuring that "there will be no poor among you, for the Lord will bless you in the land that the Lord your God is giving you for an inheritance to possess" (15:4).

Interestingly, one of the demonstrations of being righteous and blameless was to not "put out [one's] money at interest" (Psalm 15:1-5, cf. Leviticus 25:37-38).

Debt and Wisdom

Even though offering loans and the repayment of debt were permitted, ancient Biblical wisdom nonetheless strongly counseled against being on the payback side of financial obligation.
- "The rich rules over the poor, and the borrower is the slave of the lender" (Proverbs 22:7).
- "Be not one of those who give pledges, who put up security for debts. If you have nothing with which to pay, why should your bed be taken from under you?" (Proverbs 22:26-27)
- "The wicked borrows and does not pay back, but the righteous is generous and gives" (Psalm 37:21)
- Israel would be "blessed" as a lendor to other nations (Deut.

28:12), never having to borrow. Yet one of the promised curses, should Israel be disobedient to God and his Law, would be a debt enslavement to sojourning foreigners (Deut. 28:43-44). When Nehemiah arrived to rebuild a protective wall around Jerusalem, he discovered a debilitating economic situation among the people caused by borrowing, which led to selling children into slavery (Nehemiah 5:1-13).

Searching Jesus' teachings, he never explicitly condemns agreed upon arrangements of debt and repayment, but he did call for grace, wisdom, and faithfulness. In Matthew 18:23-35, he speaks of a gracious master who released several servants from overwhelming debt. In Matthew 25, he describes a present arrangement in which God's servants are entrusted with his property (i.e., in the Master's debt), and obligated to wisely invest it to make a profit (25:14-30, cf. Luke 19:11-27). Luke 7:41-43 offers a short illustration on forgiveness of debt and love.

Back To Romans 13

In all of this, a word of simple clarity which, when obeyed, offers remarkable personal freedom in the Lord. "Owe nothing to no man!"

> **THE ONLY DEBT TO WHICH WE ARE CALLED TO BE ENSLAVED IS THE OBLIGATION TO LOVE ONE ANOTHER. WE ARE LOVE-DEBTORS TO EACH OTHER.**

In its context, this directive has several important applications. For example, Christians should not be in tax debt to the government: "Pay to all what is owed to them—taxes to whom taxes are owed, revenue to whom revenue is owed, respect to whom respect is owed, honor to whom honor is owed." Jesus said, "Render to Caesar the things that are Caesar's" (Matthew 22:19-21), and himself willingly paid a temple tax (Matthew 17:24-27).

Also, the only debt we should be enslaved to is the debt to love others. "Owe nothing to no one except to love each other" (13:8), but then Paul continues. "The commandments...are summed up in this word, YOU SHALL LOVE YOUR NEIGHBOR AS YOURSELF (Lev. 19:18). Love does no wrong to a neighbor; therefore, love is the fulfilling of the Law" (13:9-10).

This posture of "no debt except to love" is especially vital to those keenly aware that our final salvation is "nearer to us now than when we first believed" (13:11), and thus the call to walk properly in the light God gives us. The Lord's return is always near-at-hand.

Let's call out debt for what it is; namely, slavery. It's entrapment results from coveting for things we want before the Lord has provided them for us. So let's wake up. Our modern economic culture, driven by the mantra-lie that one is happier if one has more things right now (!), constantly entices toward the slippery slope of easy credit and unthinking spending.

There is another way to walk in freedom, informed by wisdom and attended by joy. Work and live within your means. If you have slipped into debt, admit it and seek counsel (this humble step can be incredibly life changing!). Some surgical cancelling of credit cards may be in order.

On the positive side, start planning prayerfully and wisely, especially by putting God first in your finances. Start the regular habit of giving first to God, saving second, and spending third. Ask someone you trust to hold you accountable, and grow in smart stewardship.

By the enabling of God's Spirit, become free enough to be content in godliness with what God provides (as noted previously, He fully knows what you truly need) —

> But godliness with contentment is great gain, for we brought nothing into the world, and we cannot take anything out of the world. But if we have food and clothing, with these we will be content. (1 Timothy 6:6-8)

REFLECTION AND DISCUSSION QUESTIONS

Paul shares that he "learned in whatever situation I am in to be content...I have learned the secret of facing plenty and hunger, abundance and need" (Phil.4:11-12). What do you think is the secret of being content with what we have?

Are there any compromises with debt found in your life today? What's your plan to escape from its slavery? Are you willing to seek counsel? To be accountable?

God's steward feels a debt to love others! To whom is God calling you to show love and honor in this stretch of your life? What might God do in displaying His love through you?

TEN

MY TREASURE

Stewardship as a Family

This book began with a retelling of my father's confession to me, his son, that he had mishandled our family's finances. Truth is that back when I was growing up in my parent's home (the 1950's and 1960's), there was scant teaching even in Bible-believing churches about leading well a Christian home, much less talking with your kids about handling money.

Yet things would change. One of the significant early voices trumpeting this need was Larry Burkett, for years the director of Christian Financial Concepts. His observation?

> One of the most neglected areas of family life involves teaching children financial discipline. Even in homes where Bible study and prayer is an established way of life, finances are rarely, if ever, discussed. Is it any wonder that so many couples suffer because of financial mismanagement?
>
> But whose responsibility is it to teach children about money? In most high schools today, a consumer economics class my simply teach how to complete a credit application and not necessarily how to budget and save. If schools don't teach our children the rules of money management, who will?
>
> Often the most effective teachers are Mom and Dad, and the best lessons are learned at home. It is at home, watching a parent's example, that a child establishes lifetime habits. [However] Before parents

teach their children how to manage money, they should master the lessons themselves ("Teaching Children Financial Discipline," *Focus on the Family,* November 1984, 10-11].

Are We Willing?

If Larry Burkett helped sound the initial and important call to attention, others have followed well in his train. One can quickly find excellent, up-to-date coaching manuals for leading and discipling your tribe in Biblical stewardship.

One example is Ron Lieber's *The Opposite of Spoiled: Raising Kids who are Grounded, Generous, and Smart about Money.* This wonderfully helpful book, full of Biblical wisdom and practical child-training advice, includes chapters dealing with

- The Need to Talk about Money (with your children)
- How to Start Money Conversations
- The Allowance Debates
- The Smartest Ways for Kids to Spend
- Are We Raising Materialistic Kids
- How to Talk about Giving
- Why Kids Should Work
- The Luckiest (instilling gratitude, grace and perspective in our sons and daughters)

The values which drive this helpful resource are clearly stated:

> Finally, I want to help all of you recognize that every conversation about money is also about values. Allowance is also about patience. Giving is about generosity. Work is about perseverance. Negotiating their wants and needs and the difference between the two has a lot to do with thrift and prudence. And running through all these conversations is a desire for kids to have perspective—to know why they may have more than most people in the world. But they will probably never have more than every one of their peers. And why there's no shame in having more or having less, as long as you're grateful for what you have, share it generously with others, and spend it wisely on the things that make you happiest. It's true for our kids, but it's true for us, too. (Lieber, Ron. *The Opposite of Spoiled: Raising Kids Who Are Grounded, Generous, and Smart About Money* (p.14), HarperCollins.)

The point is that there is excellent help available to any dad, mom, or guardian to shape the values and hearts of children in line with Scripture's teaching.

Basic, Biblical Financial Principles

George Fooshee (*You Can Beat The Money Squeeze*) offers a short, helpful summary of nine key financial principles. Each could generate a helpful dinner table discussion.

- #1 GOD IS THE SOURCE of everything we have. Ask for your needs (Philippians 4:19, Proverbs 8:20-21, Romans 8:32)
- #2 GIVE proportionately, regularly, generously (Luke 6:38, 1 Corinthians 16:2, 2 Corinthians 9:7)
- #3 SAVE — the wise save for the future (Proverbs 30:24-25, 21:20, 22:3)
- #4 KEEP OUT OF DEBT — live on what you make (Proverbs 22:7, Luke 3:14, Romans 13:8)
- #5 BE CONTENT with what you have (Proverbs 5:19, Philippians 4:11-12, Hebrews 13:5)
- #6 USE RECORDS TO GUIDE PLANNING and plan ahead (Proverbs 23:23, 25:3-4, 1 Corinthians 14:40)
- #7 REFUSE TO CO-SIGN ON LOANS — a fool's choice (Proverbs 6:1-5, 11:15, 17:18, 20:16, 22:26-27, 27:13)
- #8 WORK — it's God's way for your provision (Exodus 23:12, Proverbs 14:23, 28:19, Acts 20:35, 1 Thessalonians 4:11-12)
- #9 SEEK GODLY COUNSEL — wisdom sought breeds wisdom's gains (Psalm 1:1-2, Proverbs 15:22, Romans 15:14)

Can you imagine the benefit of everyone in your family aligned around these simple practices? Sure, there will be a struggle in putting these into practice, living in an unashamedly materialistic culture. Nonetheless, the steady, prayerful practices of an intentional family can produce young disciples who experience the joys of obedience to wisdom.

Burkett noted, "These first lessons in money management (budget, give, save, only wisely borrow) are simple, but they establish habits many adults never learn. When you give your child solid financial guidelines, you give him or her a future that will be free from the bonds of excessive debt. No parent can ensure that his child will always be wise in money matters, but every parent can teach their children sound principles of financial management" (Burkett, p. 11).

In his helpful chapter on "Teaching Children about Money and Possessions" (*Money, Possessions, and Eternity*), Alcorn adds,

> The most fundamental lesson any child can learn about finances—even more important than saving—is the lesson of giving. As parents, we should teach our children to give. This is more than simply taking our own money and handing it to our child to put in the offering. In such cases the child isn't giving—she's simply delivering our gift. In order for it to really be giving, it must come from what actually belongs to the child (p.397)
> One man wrote to me, "My wife and I have taught our kids from the earliest days to be regular givers to God and his kingdom

purposes. Our family has been blessed with four young adults who love Jesus, and I believe that our faithfulness in giving has contributed to that. God's returns are not always financial."

When I asked a group to share their giving stories, one man, Daniel J. Arnold, told me, "Giving to the glory of the Lord Jesus Christ and the expansion of his kingdom on earth has become the common purpose of our family, our co-mission. We test the will of God for us in prayer and come together in agreement on every gift. Giving enters us into a life of faith and trust in God." Like everything else in the home, stewardship is caught as much as taught.

I recommend that families get involved together in special missions projects. Family members can work together to financially support, pray for, and correspond with a missionary, a needy family, or an overseas orphan. Becoming aware of needs elsewhere reminds our children of the incredible abundance in America and our opportunity to share it with the needy (p.398-399).

So, what fresh steps are you willing to take with your family? No doubt God's Spirit himself will be eager to empower the leadership you provide (cf. Ephesians 3:14-19). Perhaps your sincere, generous obedience can impact your sons and daughters the way my father's obedience so deeply influenced me. To God be the glory.

REFLECTION AND DISCUSSION QUESTIONS

A person's or couple's willingness to intentionally disciple their children in financial matters may depend on whether or not their own parents did this. What was your experience? What did you learn from your parents about money?

How would you like to improve on what your parents did (or did not do) in this area?

Is there an insight from this chapter that struck an important chord in your thinking? If so, what difference will that make in how you view and use money going forward?

GENEROSITY AND KINGDOM INVESTING

For many fruitful years, Dr. Chris Dolson ably led Blackhawk (EFC) Church in Madison, Wisconsin. Of the many factors making that body of believers a kingdom force in the Midwest, a key was their pastor's clear teaching on a lifestyle of generosity. In his helpful booklet, *Generosity*, Chris spotlights how the Apostle Paul personally modeled the directive of his Lord: "In everything I did, I showed you that by this kind of hard work we must help the weak, remembering the words the Lord Jesus Himself said, 'It is more blessed to give than to receive'" (Acts 20:35 [NIV]).

The booklet brings to light, and wonderfully illustrates, that generosity is a matter of the heart.

"Generosity" derives from the Latin word generous, which means "of noble birth." That Latin word was passed down to English through the Old French word generous, later genereux ("noble, magnanimous"). Most recorded English uses of the word "generous" up to and during the 16th century reflect an aristocratic sense of being of noble birth. To describe someone as being generous was literally a way of saying they belonged to nobility. During the 18th century, the meaning of "generosity" continued to evolve in directions that we are more familiar with today. The word began to denote the concepts of open-handedness and liberality in giving money and possessions to others. Over the centuries in the English-speaking world, the word "generosity" developed from describing people of an elite class to an admirable quality that could be practiced by anyone with a noble character (cf. Smith, C. & Davidson, H., (2014), The Paradox of Generosity, 3.)

Today, generosity is considered the virtue of giving good things to others freely and abundantly. To be generous means that one is liberal with one's "stuff" (time, talent, and treasures) to others. Generous people don't keep count or track things; they just give freely and abundantly. You get that sense that nothing could make them happier.

A young woman in our church once explained that feeling to me. A divorced mother of three small children, working as a waitress in Madison, she decided on her own to give all of her tip money away to help others. She told me with tears in her eyes that at first she didn't know if she could do it. But she noticed that the more she gave away, the more tips she started to receive. She was so filled with joy that she just had to come and tell me. She was experiencing what Jesus said, "It is more blessed to give than to receive."

Generous believers, Chris notes, put into practice by the power of the Holy Spirit "some basic principles that sound strange to the rest of the world."

- **Generous people believe that everything really belongs to God.**
  Psalm 24:1 "The earth is the Lord's and everything in it, the world and all who live in it."
- **Generous people are content with God's current provision for their lives.**
  1 Timothy 6:6-8 "But godliness with contentment is great gain. For we brought nothing into the world, and we can take nothing out of it. But if we have food and clothing, we will be content with that."
- **Generous people have a giving plan.**
  2 Corinthians 9:7 "Each of you should give what you have decided in your heart to give, not reluctantly or under compulsion, for God loves a cheerful giver."
- **Generous people plan for the future.**
  Proverbs 6:6-8 "Go to the ant, you sluggard, consider its ways and be wise! It has no commander, no overseer or ruler, and yet it stores its provisions in the summer and gathers its food at harvest."

Those at Christ Community Church (Ames, Iowa) find a kinship call to generosity as a key practice that connects others to life-defining relationships in Christ. Living in humble, obedient relationship with our Lord and with one another, we desire to express "radical generosity; that is, to live adventurously to impact our world. The life question, "How are my investments doing?" along with accompanying evaluation questions, help to benchmark where we now are, and also how we might grow in generosity.

LIFE QUESTION #6: HOW ARE MY INVESTMENTS DOING?

FOCUS:	Invest in Christ's mission with time, talents, and treasure
CORE PRINCIPLE:	Generous stewardship of my time, talent, and treasure brings joy
BIBLICAL REFERENCES:	Ephesians 5:15-16, Matthew 25:23, Matthew 6:21; also Luke 12:13-32, Matthew 25:14-30, Romans 12:3-8
EVALUATIVE QUESTIONS:	■ What might God be telling me about how I use my time? My gifts and talent? My money? ■ When I look back over my life, what would make me wonder if I stored up too many treasures on earth? ■ How am I serving in my church? In my community? In the world?

Evaluation-Growth Tool

Scoring   1=never   2=seldom   3=occasionally   4=frequently   5=regularly

My bank account reflects my investments in a heavenly kingdom	1 2 3 4 5
I regularly serve people in a ministry at Christ Community Church	1 2 3 4 5
I pray and financially support a missionary/missionary family	1 2 3 4 5
I serve my community in a specific way to enhance the gospel's reputation	1 2 3 4 5
I go out of my way to show love to people I meet	1 2 3 4 5
I sacrificially contribute my finances to help others in the church and community	1 2 3 4 5
I understand my spiritual gifts and use those gifts to serve others	1 2 3 4 5
I serve others expecting nothing in return	1 2 3 4 5
I invest some time each week on spiritually investing in Christ-centered life-defining relationship interactions with others	1 2 3 4 5
Meeting the needs of others provides a sense of joy and purpose in my life	1 2 3 4 5

Simple, periodic and prayerful evaluation before the Lord, and setting new goals can facilitate a growing life-style of adventurous generosity toward others. It can be used by the Spirit of God to lovingly bring others to life in the Savior.

ACKNOWLEGEMENTS

The challenge afforded me during the 2017-2020 ministry years, to offer 60-70 day devotional guides and readers for Christ Community Church, has truly been a humbling one. This gracious church has eagerly welcomed each publication with the joy of God's Spirit. May the Lord continue to use these devotionals. They encourage rhythms for using CCC's life questions, shaping how we know and depend on God's Spirit, experiencing joy in His presence, authentically walking together with the Lord Jesus, and being fruitful in the mission of connecting people to life-defining relationships in Christ.

	Life Question	Devotional Guide
#1	Is the Spirit flowing through me?	Engage the Spirit
#2	Does God make my day?	Experience His Presence
#3	Who shares my tough stuff?	A Cord of Three Strands
#4	How worn is my welcome mat?	Winsome—Loving to Share the Good News
#5	With whom am I fishing?	Choose Greatness—Serve!
#6	How are my investments doing?	Where Your Treasure Is

I am deeply grateful for several fellow servants instrumental in encouraging and fashioning this devotional reader — Wayne Stewart, Derek Hanson, Andy Rohrback, and Pamela Staff.

Unless otherwise noted, all Scripture quotations are taken from the English Standard Version (ESV), 2001 © Crossway (a publishing ministry of Good New Publishers, ESV Text Edition 2016).

This devotional reader is dedicated in honor of our parents — Donald and Mary Ellen Staff, and A. Bruce and Lois MacRae — who were always truly generous in sacrificial love and giving. They gave themselves first to the Lord (2 Corinthians 8:5), and then to their children, family, the work of the Lord, and hundreds upon hundreds of others. We bless the Lord for them, and we cannot thank them enough.

Pamela and David Staff
January 2021